Moonrise

To Ben, Charlie, Dan & Seamus

"The mullet is the reason why people hate you"
— Wesley Willis

MEIRION JORDAN
Moonrise

seren

Seren is the book imprint of
Poetry Wales Press Ltd.
57 Nolton Street, Bridgend, Wales, CF31 3AE
01656 663018
www.seren-books.com

ISBN 978-1-85411-481-5

A CIP record for this title is available from the British Library.

The publisher acknowledges the financial assistance of the Welsh Books Council.

Cover painting by Gareth Hugh Davies: 'Procession/Gorymdaith' (detail)

Printed in Bembo by Bell & Bain, Glasgow

Contents

Calculus

I have been wearing the rhythms of the sea
all day, the swing of it rising in my arms,
my fingers scathing the backwash
for the solidus of flat stones, raising them
firm as words in my fist and then
pitching their ellipses back,
their shadows meeting them as they kiss
the meniscus over and over with the lightness
of an eclipse. The wavefronts
hardly gulp as they go under but already
I have thrown another, skimming it
further, each one further over the sea,
over the universe's edge, their arcs
extending as they skip into the gaps between stars.
Stones you can't ignore. And here behind me
I might have a crowd, an idler dragging out
the dogend of the day. Probably none.
I will be here 'til the beachcombers are gone,
the massive sun washed up on the horizon.
The sunbathers depart. The swimmers.
Soon I will be alone. Tonight
I will be out late, then very late,
turning my pebbles at the spinning moon.

Poppy field

October, you slaked the dry furrows with grain
and June the fields came blistering with poppies,
winking their black eyes in the breeze. Walking
the field ditch now it is as though the hedge extends
a rain of hands snatching the light, as though the earth
leaves you the bruise of foxgloves, a septicaemia
of primrose, an unintended gift. And from the hill's scalp
down to where the river rattles in the limestone's throat
the slope gushes with fists, blood red, grasping black eyes.

The new world

Roll on global warming. The Maentwrog Junta
seizing power on a Sunday morning
just after chapel, the frenziedly moustachioed
General Gwydion Mendéz proclaiming martial law
after the third psalm of the evening service.
The Gorseinon drugs cartel expanding
to the Aberystwyth favelas, bringing the clash
of kalashnikovs to constitution hill.
Samba and harps. O Seion Fryn
bawled out at thirty in the shade
by sweating ministers. Cawl mango
and coconuts replacing lava bread. Ronaldinho Davies
wowing the crowds at the Millennium Stadium,
the Rhondda turning out in rainbows
of rippling cloth and streamers to see England lose
four-nil, Islwyn Marley at half time
shaking the stands with sounds from Ynys Môn.
Olwen Perón leading the mob in Marchog Iesu
at the Cwmdonkin bandstand, her voice
spreading like an angelus along
the Taff Fechan, along Cwm Tywi.
David Attenborough filming the fauna
of the Nantgwynant valley, eccentric Englishmen
looking for the lost city of Dolgellau
up Cwm Pennant, out behind Corris.
100 percent humidity at Rhandirmwyn.
Kurtz Jenkins on the shores of Llyn Clywedog,
and everything from Llanidloes to Rhaeadr
declared 'the dark interior'. The rattan
wrapping itself around the spine of the A470,
the cobalt lizards and the coral snakes
swallowing the cottages at Llandinam,
the mahoganies uprooting Carno's hearths.
The moon at Devil's Bridge pulled earthwards
in a sail of vines, the sun
squinting in the eye of a bromeliad
that wields its universe of frogspawn out
from Carnedd Dafydd to the new world.

Girl on a motorbike in India

for Katharine

Here, straddling the surge of a two-stroke,
your hips hovering over a grubby pillion
at every jolt of the dirt road, where the trees
throw up their trunks to holler back at you
the engine's racket, and every thicket
wants you for a bride –

Here, where your mouth's smudged
to a go-faster stripe and the wind rushes in
on your shouts, you fly your hair
like a flag, and the afternoon's turbocharger
whips you downhill, gathering speed –

Here, shouldering through blurred villages
on the whiff of gasoline, and your voice
urges headlong into the dazzling river –

Here you are weightless, and light's fingers
are too slow in reaching you. Your knuckles

whiten. Your heart flexes its red wings.

Circe and Odysseus

Circe in spring fingers
the iron bedstead, scratches the paint
to ten years back, to Odysseus
moving on that mattress, his hands
clasping and clasping at those stains,
his hair tossing in the pulse
of their blood, his tendons shivering.
All that last night he lashed,
then put before the wind:
before his sail was swallowed
under the curve of the horizon,
her hair was already tied back,
the house stood open to the vines
that month on month invited themselves in.
Lately she has been walking on the beach:
her toes swing sand across the tiles
each time she comes indoors.
Too much, now,
she sits on the iron bed-frame
picking at the bare rigging
of its springs. And too often
she remembers his silence that year,
how each ripple of him bore
into her racing fingers
only one word, Ithaca.

The insular minuscules

I.

I found an angel in a scoop of rock:
whitening in my back yard its bones proved
fulmar, their shadows tilting in the breeze.

II.

However far from here the moon
is a tracery where saints appear
burning and white as feathers.

III.

Down a long tunnel I cannot hear
their voices raised over the white
horses, the racing bones of the sea.

IV.

And waking at midnight the scuffle
of something perched inside my brain.
I wait. To hear it move again.

V.

Let me consult the gospels of the body:
the book of the lungs. The carpet page
of the mind. The picked-clean frets of the spine.

VI.

This was a garden. This is a tide
of chicory and daisies rising over it.
This a scriptorium. This a proper of time.

VII.

Northwestern light and heavy lintels,
the hills keeping their broadcast
into the centuries ahead.

VIII.

I too see angels and shearwaters
climbing to the edge of vision between
ruined clouds, ascending, descending.

IX.

And all earth peopled with the work
of another millennium. Tiny figures. Diminishing.
Angel, I'm trying to return your calls.

X.

The needle dithering. A cantus firmus. A sign
you're coming through. The looped transmission.
You were my news. This is the northern sky.

Another poem about living on Mars

This was our day out through tinted goggles:
our shoes stinting on rock, the track of us landing
over snaggled cliffs, an ocean of dust rocking
there into our hands. We smiled and waved
so hard we might have had six arms, six heads.
Then lunch among gypsum daisies, our fingers
tracing the ancient watercourses like conversations.
And tonight, watching the plastic vegetation rusting
in the wind, the polyester cycads and bromeliads
shaking, I wished for rain in purple clouds rotting
through the red crust on olives, a red rain darkening the soil,
drenching and dashing and ceaseless.

The Nuclear Disaster Appreciation Society

Wonderland, for me, was that place in Nevada
that they built, and then blew up:
a holocaust of mannequins scrambled into ions.
That got me started, and watching Hiroshima
go up in forty-five my friend Dave said
"that's beautiful video," and it was.
Hence the society. We got together
for the evening news from Three-Mile Island,
partied the half-lives away after Chernobyl.
We had a day out once, to Windscale:
tea in a thermos and the North Sea
flavouring our sandwiches from miles off.
But we don't get out so much these days,
watch the classics on DVD at weekends.
Muroa, maybe, or one of those Pacific places
at any rate. We love to watch
the palm trees beating in the thorium breeze,
the rising heart of the cloud
like sunshine in our eyes:
from that mushrooming somewhere
our laughter comes like a chain reaction,
starts with a chuckle,
melts down into the world.

Sky writing

for Nina

I know a girl who can read skies like novels,
can understand that filigree of brilliance, one hand
held up feeling it like Braille: for her
an open window is a monograph
and glass a fabulous retelling. She says
that rain is always heartfelt, fog
a gripping read and walks, palms upward,
smiling, in the sleet. Some days
I call to find her sitting on the roof
engrossed, unpicking the errata of a jet stream
or considering interpretations in a mirror.
She sits outside for weeks on end in summer
and says she'll teach me someday. But I
don't know quite where to start, so mostly
I just pour the tea and watch her read.
Lately, though, she has been standing
in high places. I'm afraid one day
I'll find inside a minaret or spire
a pair of her unneeded shoes, and then I'll know
she's gone to scrawl her thoughts on the ionosphere
trailing vapour like a Saturn Five, leaving her mark
among the bright calligraphy of clouds.

The wasp queen

she will not sleep.
her wings trouble the glass
seeking the heat,
my breath. her lips are moist,

her wings trouble the glass:
they dwindle on
my breath. her lips are moist;
like mine they part

and dwindle on
the whiteness of my skin.
like mine they part,
those gleaming legs against

the whiteness of my skin.
she frets, her sting,
her gleaming legs against
me. she crawls in.

she frets, she stings.
she will not sleep.
me, she crawls in
seeking the heat.

Head of an athlete in an Ionian shipwreck

Like two lovers laughing we surface
from the sea's kiss: my hand a stethoscope,
I can still hear it crashing in the cave
of your chest, the waves on Kassos.
Far down the sea tugs at us still,
the lobed seaweed and the lolling squid
begging us back, down into the blue dark,
our masks gasping into us as we
go diving on the wreck, its hull yawed up,
our hands divining cargoes of wrought marble,
silt. And still that youth looks out
from windowless sand, his eyes serene and blank:
down there his smile is white as alum,
inviting as a blue infinity of fish. And already
I can feel my body tilting to him like a level, already
we are going down again and perfectly still
we fly into the blue silence like stones.

The Magdalen College chef

Flesh red as blood
bleeding under fingers,
he knows it all: pepper stalks
curling on his thumb, cream
bursting in the pan. His steel
flashes in the small hours
for moments like this, his tendons
curdled with exercise, paring moths
on the wing. His knives
bare bream bones, the full hearts
of tomatoes, sometimes
a careless knuckle. But it's worth it:
his ratatouille turns
on a spun heel, his soufflés
bloom from a dipped fork.
Upstairs his ragouts seethe
under the grins of dons and demons
and his hymns of cardamom
are sipped at by divines.
He's unconcerned. All Souls' he crawls
out from the cradle of the hob's flare
to stand under that dark shaking
of bells, his butts
skittering their fire over the quad,
the stars a rain of sparks.
His blown smoke beckons
something in him past Mary
clutching at her cauliflower child,
some black thing aching
to arch itself beyond
sproutings of angels unfurling their florets
towards a seedling moon.

Blockbuster season

Antihero (A) inserts tongue (B)
into mouth of starlet (C), menacing villain
(K) with weapon (M). Meanwhile
Steve Buscemi plots my brother's jailbreak
and on his moonbase Ming the Merciless unveils
his doomsday cannon. Car chases ensue,
Darth Vader using my Ford Fiesta to escape
from Colditz and the set of Grease.
Dick Dastardly is chasing Hugh Grant
in a mini through Turin, my first kiss
leaves Scarlett O'Hara breathless but Clint Eastwood
knocks the king-size popcorn from my hand.
The projectionist is playing
K Billy's Super Sounds of the Seventies
and the Dambusters go in for their final run,
Dresden is burning, as is Stalingrad,
the White House and the alien attack fleet,
the Enterprise, the universe, the cinema:

the bins and gutters fill; this film
I have been watching all my life.
Sonrisos Nachos float like islands in the rain.

The astronomer's wife

The year the doves nested on the lens
of my telescope I went outside
to find my wife sitting in constellations
of blossom, the lawn shining with petals.

And though, under the umbra of my dome,
sieving the sky for patterns in the night,
I only dreamed of her, slim fingers
spinning a garden from the alien flowers,

hearing my footsteps bend the grass
her face rose like a moon from seas
of hydrangeas. Watching me squint
into my first seconds of May her eyes

grew wide as an instrument dial
or a sky full of astronauts. She smiled.

The parks in flood

The ice-cream man threatens the ducks
with his institutional shadow, the oaks open
and the week's first suicide spins from his rope.

Here comes the professor sweeping over ripples
on his lilo, the doctor following in her neon waders.
All swans and tower blocks pile on sail,

the bag lady is barefoot on drowned grass.
Atlantis lies shin-deep and on a horizon by Paul Klee
the benches are a flotilla where cormorants sit

and dip their beaks into the weekend news.

Rosamund's tomb

No effigy in attitude of prayer,
no masses said, no place in the parade
of graven dead, the centuries of care
vanished like footsteps down the colonnade,

no skeins of pilgrims treading up the aisles
clasping their gifts and rosaries to thread
their hands through one another as the miles
of daylight rest over your tempered head:

only the meadow and the crumpled stone,
the weeping hedges and the meadow grass
know where you sleep. The pilgrims gone,
the rain processes like the cadence of a mass

over the hallowed floors you used to pace,
then passes, as all things are meant to pass.

Pirate music

Jazz up your GTIs with spoilers,
subs and stereos then cane it down the ringroad,
windows open with your mates
bouncing to dancehall, hip hop, what the fuck
will take your fancy on a Friday night.
And make it wild. Get in a few
down at the Wetherspoons, then join the crew
for Aftershocks and Breezers somewhere
with a jukebox just to get the juices
flowing, bring your peeps out on their feet,
then take it down the club, your mates
knocking back Bud and braying ghetto, getting down
to Fiddy Cent and Dizzee, eyeing up
the talent, getting lucky getting
laid and leaving early with some fitty
who will grope them in a taxi,
fuck then fuck off home. Saturday
you don't get up 'til twelve and you
get KFC for breakfast, play some Gamecube,
PS2, visit the missus or your mum,
go down the pool hall then the pub,
watch all the thugs get drunk then tear it up
just like last night but more, more drinks
more drugs more razzle dazzle and more dirty beats.
Sunday. Mind your head and maybe chill
with DVDs or downloads, see the family
and psych yourself for Monday and another week
of temping, selling, fucking, all the shit that
gets you through to the weekend. With luck
you'll do it all for years to come. It's pirate music, yours
because you took it and you'll dance
and drink and screw to it, be cool to it,
but all this time keep moving to it
past the rec, the Tescos, the estate, back down
the ringroad past the crematorium and out

into the unfamiliar brightness of the fields.

Hawthorns blossoming

I move like stage scenery:
thinly, on wheels. Birds
think I skim up the slope
into a blue mouth of cloud.
And here they are again,
God's last doodles for man
letting out their parachutes
for the freefall weather. Come,
they are saying, even the black
wood can be whited
with scrags of sheep's wool,
tearings of carrier bags,
vaseline, mist:
over their shoulders
my drenching rushes downhill.
My umbrella opening
blots out the flowers.

Dyddgu

Dyddgu, I remember
the drowned woman at Llangors,
how they pulled her
unprotesting, blue at the lips,
to the shore.

That year Llyn-Y-Fan froze
and I touched the heel of my palm
to the ice, hoping to hear you knocking
from the far side,
the vibrations spreading to me
from the lake's deep centre.

Who crosses the surface of the water
crosses into legend. I hear the Myddfai
under the black tarns of the hills,
Culhwch and Olwen staring
into the looped videotape of the sky.

The pools in winter fill
with the pre-recorded dead,
history's answerphones:
Dyddgu, even you are no longer listening.

Your reply will only be
a masterwork of silent cinema,
that one long shot of you
smiling and mouthing
as a producer holds against the lens
a series of blank cards.

Strategikon

Their marginalia impinge over the moonlight's scroll,
the men and exoskeletons discarded on the plain:
here's John Doukas smiling on the evening's prospect
where the axe has bared his sympathetic teeth;
here Constantine Diogenes disputes an arrow's logic,
a rhetoric of larvae embellishing his throat;
and there Botaniates lays his damask to the earth
as tenderly as he laid out his groves in Epirus.
Guiscard here, and Bohemond his son repose
in hauberks as they did at home, and here too dogs
and falcons reach over their outstretched limbs:
here many hands extend on Anatolia's page,
twitching in histories of dust. Here eyes and tongues
are fixed in praise for dynasties of ants.

The Sunday Adventure Club

I see them sometimes, even now,
the mute girl hoicking a pushchair
uphill, against the wind,
the crippled kid behind the tills at Tescos,
the however-many of them hurrying
separately over dim car parks,
heads down, or over rain-slashed streets.
Except for him. Sometimes I watch
a shadow waiting for a bus,
a reflection gangling past shop windows
that reminds me of how I first saw them,
the breeze singing in the spokes
of my upturned bicycle, my head
just poking from the summer ditch
to catch him striding over the playing fields,
them straggling after, even the freckled one
I picked on in year six and the fat kid
whose lunch money bought me my cigarettes.
Just after that the signs appeared
tacked onto lampposts or under
the photographs of girls in phone kiosks:
Sunday Adventure Club. Behind the old cement works.
Twelve o'clock. I never went,
but followed them that August
through a fly-tippers' wonderland,
trying to spot them through the stands
of brambles, knotweed, chain-link fences,
between the clumps of sheds by the canal.
Not that I caught them. Nor in the month
of Sundays after: all that I saw was him
drawing them on into the skyline over rubble,
bombsites, lanes clenched with thorns or slag.
Rain or the council took their signs down years ago
but they are still here, still peering on
into the grubby distance, hoping for a shadow
passing over the broken ground,
all joints. Perhaps he moved away.
Last January I found the den, a stream
angling a gulley from woods

that might have been theirs, a few
tin sheets laced up with wire, a black circle
of stones where tramps had lit their fires, snow
sprinkled like broken glass, a swing.
He isn't coming back there, they
have been ten years laying low. Still
what adventures they had, I don't know.

Lazarus

You smell me. I
have been underground
out in the woods,
sightless, breathing loam.
I did not sleep
or dream until your hand
found mine among
the leaf-litter and hauled
my six-weeks-cold
body back to light.
And how you breathe
me, sniffing the mould
flowering at the angles
of my skin, the soft
footprints of beetles
nestling in my back.
How rich, you say,
how deep as organ music
your smell is.
You peel moss
from my chest, kissing
the blue-veined flesh.
You place your mouth
on mine, siphon
the black odours from
my mouth:
how I would kiss you
if this earth did not
well from my mouth.

Downstream from Catraeth

the heron dips its beak
to a flickering river,

white gulls fill a broad sky
over reed-beds.

A herdsman tends kine
down a wisp of track, finds

a brooch, iron, its pin broken,
firewood, a warrior floating,

and a torque of gold.

Still life

Because she wanted the colours of evening on the tops
of buildings, the ones she couldn't name, and got
grey afternoons swilling in her water glass and husks

of conversations from the strangers in the street,
the handful of snowdrops lifting their cool tongues
from the lawn, pursing their roots against the step,

reminded her of her last lover, the asian boy whose lips
bloomed over hers, his fingers searching for her
like the scraps of moonlight between curtains. Each night

she dreamed of white rooms where she heard the snowdrops
murmur in the cold, so she took pity. All that raw week
they dripped their petals on her desk, their edges crinkling,

showing their dry veins. But for a month the sun
opened on the shadowed angles of the terraces
and she found words for it, vermilion and saffron,

jasper and ultramarine, as frost waking on the sketches
of trees or in low ground rises, wears colours again.

All my friends

for John Fuller

The first drops, nudging the tired air
and they are here again,
stepping from the voids each raindrop leaves
behind it as the weather breaks and sky
at last batters the parched ground.
Nothing is recognised. However often
they might make this journey
back to us, they soon forget
out in their lonely arks and so I see them now,
bartering for scraps of conversation
with the crows, kneeling in the shafts
of brightness that prop up spaces between clouds,
their hands clasped and their lips
sipping extravagant light: they are all here,
Dyer, Drayton, Dowland, all my friends,
drinking this gift of woods and buttercups
with tongues as slight as cobwebs.
And as the rain slackens, so their bare feet
lift, slowly at first then soaring they
climb back into nothing and the ears
of grass sway, as if catching prayers.

Saints of the African church

I.
But they never left their rock-cut churches for some eternal city.
Once every few decades an Abuna would come from distant
Alexandria where the Patriarch looked not south but east and
north and west to Tyre, to Antioch, to far Byzantium. Their
world, it seemed, hung on a silver thread of Nile. Each time their
new Archbishop came, his feet still dusty from the long, dry
road, he would see the octagonal chapels where the people
prayed to a Christ of water and daylight, and give thanks to two
natures unified in icons of red stone.

II.
Not for them the mappa mundi, the imperial sphere re-centred
on the holy city. In Lalibela the twelve churches were cut from
the mountain and named for sights few Ethiopians could hope
to see. Bete Golgotha, Bete Amanuel, the word sprang into
being at each tapping of the masons' chisels. And why turn in
faith towards Galilee, or to the Latins clustering around a shad-
ow falling on the Tyrrhenian sea, where galleys breathed on
crescent-handed waves, when Christ and the Virgin had walked
among the hills at Muja, and the covenant burned in its golden
ark in ancient Aksum?

III.
The Latin world looks in. Loyola had feared them damned, the
League of Nations listened to Salassie's speeches and did noth-
ing. The Pope has always dreamed of a messiah with a moon
face, his halo bright and true as a coin.

IV.
In Carthage and Hippo, Cyrene and Lepcis Magna, the iconers
paint Christ black against acacia panels. Augustine sleeps with
his dark-skinned woman through the hot Saturday afternoons,
resting his hand over his lover's thigh. Is this his dream, the green
hill-country where a Madonna murmurs in Ge'ez, the
Evangelists let water fall on unbaptised earth? At three a.m.
when Augustine turns over in sleep, I wake. I watch him disap-
pear into the distance ahead of me, an old man walking uphill
through snow.

Home, 1919

He sees it now, flooding
in evening light over the copperworks,
up Balaclava street, up Sebastopol drive,
into the blushes of his wife's face
after sex. And spreading
to albums, to orchids pressed
between suppurating pages,
to photographs of summer, 1912,
the colour of it, dried.
He finds his books
uncomfortable, their spines
sticky to touch, the crimson plush
of theatres quivering, rippled.
Just whose he cannot say.
Jenkins', is it? Or Davies',
whose sons still clatter
hobnails up the cobbled hills
to a bundle of scrawled letters,
the worn blinds down.
It could be worse, he thinks,
he could still pace
his sector of the front at night,
or flatten, prone,
at every slamming door.
At least now he finds company
in his nicked skin, shaving,
in his rows of hyacinths urging
their hundreds of red faces sunwards,
the insects nuzzling
at their slick lips.

HMS Ark Royal in action

after the watercolour by Eric Ravilious

Toy ships glued against a model sea.
No flak: the bombers twirling
indifferent as fireflies. Above,

the moon torpedoed, listing.
Already it is capsizing
from the sky. Out on the fleet

signal lamps click and twitter.
Searchlights feathering the surface
pick out the few cormorants,

sea-birds. Three o'clock. A shoal
of star-shells going up. Beyond:
night, water. Squadrons of stars.

Cry wolf

Once I was told that long ago
there were no poems, only wolves.
Poets would spend weeks
by the winter hearth, sharpening bone
until it grinned in the firelight,
splitting flints down to the last vowel.
Then as the night filled with snow
they would go out like ghosts through the woods
and return with great snarling pelts,
some of which can still be seen.
It is safer now. Nobody
loses an eye or a hand
to metaphor these days. And though
some people, in the high Carpathians
or among the Urals' snaggled vertebrae
claim to have seen the real thing,
most bring back dog skin, badly dyed.
Now we gaze hungrily
through the windows of museums
at the crooked smiles and glass eyes,
the weave of dust that was wolves:
in a few towns you can queue
down corridors of fishbowl glass
for your chance to shoot their relics.

Ecce homo

"A shadow is a man
when the mosquito death approaches."

— Keith Douglas

Douglas I can hear it, the drizzle of wings
from somewhere among these machines, a whine
subversive as the drip in the vein. Look. His weight
hardly disturbs the level of the hospital bed,
his limbs wasted to wrinkles in the blankets.
And now the insect lands, inhabits him,
spreading its plethora of legs in algorithms that
defy superstition. Here is the man of chitin,
the black rhythms of arms and hooks tangling
and multiplying under the sheets. That thin sound
is the mosquito swarming where a voice should be.
It stops. The nurses come
and smooth the shadow from the bed's white stone.

Hinterlands

I. The radio

tuned in to us in the night and left us staring,
static-eyed. Its tales of cities
floating on light and other stubs
of legends from that dead language
lured us to reply. For months
we stammered the lacunae of morse
to their transmitter but still we heard
its broadcast in the closed rooms of sleep.
Even the dead chattered with signal,
their hearts startled to a mains hum.
It called us home. The provinces
were needed now, it said, return
to your eternal city. We set out.
Dawn of our second day we reached
the high ridge overshadowing our valley.
Compasses swung true. We saw for miles.

II. Hinterlands

Nearer now we picked out details:
flowers drowning the hayfields,
skies fenced in with wires.
We saw the enemy flocking in dark clouds
on the horizon and we understood.
The woods grew thinner here, we traced
the rusted palisades beside the railway lines
to guide us on. Hiding at night
the frequency swelled inside our brains,
the voices louder in a language that
we barely parsed, a few archaic sentences
we grasped and turned over in our dreams.
At last we came on gardens, concrete walks,
a river, even ribs of boats. We knew
how close we were: our skulls vibrated
to the radio's pitch. We picked our way
through weeds and brambles, the sun
screeching, the moon blaring down.
A few deer startled at our approach.

III. Artifacts

But on the sixtieth day we find
ourselves to be breaking up.
The radio talks through us. We make
many new discoveries each hour
but some die from disease. We lay them
to eternal rest among the Betamax,
pray for their souls to remain in VHS
forever. The enemy have become
our shadows in the suburbs at night;
their smiles lengthen in the dialect
of mirrors. Ten thousand miles down
our city bathes in radiation, the eyes
descend to it at dawn like bathyspheres.
Sun screeching still, moonlight
extending its piers over water. The static
trails over the columns of our brains. It blooms.
Our tongues are pinned by its aerial thorns.

IV. Inscriptions

"The invaders eat only human flesh"
                    – Andrew Waterhouse

Where we invaders come from
it is all two up, two down:
each house must hinge open on demand
and the inhabitants parade in period dress.

All mail is now administered
by the war graves commission:
only the dead may send
or open letters. Our young
are shrink-wrapped and delivered to war
in a distant country, to think of them
condemns the soul to auction.

The cities wait deserted for our final triumph;
we wait like cenotaphs along the sides
of green hills. Enlightenment has given us
new language, ten thousand syllables of silence.

All this our God vouchsafed to us.
He stands above us empty as the streets at noon.

Vampire

"I'm a vampire, baby" – Mercury Rev

But I'm a vampire, baby,
everything you've ever wanted:
the sixteenth century, the music
of nocturnal hemispheres, girls,
guns and freedom
from the blue fandango of your fears.

Which is what I am now. I'm the prickling hairs
in closed rooms before the light clicks on,
the red dream of your father. I'm
sniffing you out in monochrome:
watch closely and you'll catch
my nose twitching into wolf-space,
my cells dissembling until I'm mist.
Nosferatu? Don't make me laugh.
I'm not running the comfortable rails
those old stories provide:
I'm a bat when it suits me,
not when it would be –
dramatic. Your blood shows up
on sonar. I can lurk
down in the crypt of your mind
with the best of them, baby,
and I come to life in the century
of my choosing. Yes, I feed,
but you and me aren't symbionts:

locked up in the shadows of my castle
I only need to look into a mirror
and I am reaching over the one-atom gap
to where you and I are circling,
closer and closer,
in the frost of that next room.

The Birnbeck elegy

D. M. Jones, 1914-2008

I.

Sleepless for once, now he is quiet,
she hears his bed stutter from the other room
and then resume its breathing.
The windowsill carries its bloom

of arc-lights and peroxide flowers
from the hospital that backs on
behind the laurels. She hears the throb
of pumps keeping his body still

where sometimes he drifts and clutches
at the bedframe, gulping for
her name: Joan, where sometimes she
will rise and watch him, frayed

in her nightdress, and place the palm
of her hand against him; but not this night.

II.

Tear down the water-chute and switchback rides,
dismantle What The Butler Saw and let
no slide-show booth or stall disturb the fret
of night waves, on the pier island, at high tide.

Shut up the bioscope and odeon,
and lead the donkeys from the evening sand:
cancel the matinees; nor Tom Mix, nor Sol Vang
will fill tuppenny seats at thruppence-with-plums.

Let there be quiet, and the white paint rusting
from balustrades. Let the constellations
gaze on clear decking, the wind blustering

from North-West: Lord, let only your hand
rain the afternoon tea of consolations,
and once a week the British Legion band.

A short visit to the psychiatrist

You tell me that it's not
the alien bacteria, the scientist
with robot arms pursuing you,
the son of the industrialist you killed
screaming revenge outside the window
of your dingy flat that have been keeping you
awake. It was arachnophobia
that left your sheets a lake of sweat,
a web of muscle tightening
and tightening over your chest.
Your bed became a freefall
between tower blocks, you say,
your only safety net
unfortunately silk, and sticky.
I think you're lying, spiderman,
that the concentric ripples of events
don't have you at their centre — a case
in point: you claim you're Peter
Parker under that mask. Not so.
I've been the one wearing distinctive
webbing after dark, engaging
villains in an aerial ballet as vicious
as it was exhilarating. You
have been cocooned here all this time,
living off micro-ready meals
and the patience of your landlord.
You should get out more. Try
holding a normal conversation.
Learn jazz guitar, or visit galleries,
and try not to look quite so surprised
when I descend, eight-legged,
from the roof. This is
for your own good. I cannot help you
if you won't accept the truth.

Scharnhorst

After the water closed and the smoke dispersed
they picked the men, white, out of a shivering sea:
so many voices led off blindfold into the past
that I can hardly claim to hear. But at night
I think of the radio operator, still at his set
as the water rushes round the bulkhead
into his last message, five fathoms down,
a sound like scratching, scratching at the door
that keeps him out, the static: Ich. Ich.

The owls

In February Mark began to grow a beak.
Nose and jaw meshed, hardening,
orbits expanded to the two discs of a face.
Somehow his eyes deepened and his head learnt
to turn in ever increasing arcs:
He was the first to go. Then Aled,
breath misting on the sight of his shock-white plumage
one evening in the mirror,
flapped himself through the bathroom window
and returned by hag-light with a throat full of vole.
Two weeks later I found Sam and Marie
preening each other in my hay-loft,
heard the low hooting and the scuffle of sharp feet.
I knew it. My neighbours were turning into owls.
At first I thought nothing of it, except that my barns
stank of the cold sweat of mice each morning,
I grew used to the ghost of wings crossing my windows,
eyes gliding in the woods after dark.
Then solitary populations retreated to their attics
and my street became a gust of boarded doorways,
gales hunted over the empty fields.
Now each dusk I watch them rise
through the skeletons of the old roofs and listen
to tufted ears pricking the silence. In winter
the houses rise windowless into a blear sky,
an owls' citadel of rafters and roosts.
And each night I sit under the last lamp in the house
hearing the clink and rasp of their claws at the slate,
each night I dream of snow under a huge moon,
my shadow broad and beating it like down.

A camera at Senghenydd pit

I. Negatives

But there were scenes I did not capture, men
grottoed like statues underground, the smoke's
slow wringing of their lungs or that one searing
flash. The dead were brought out only in the flesh,

but in that instant shadows agonized
over the rock that reached blue, living air
and shook the tin-roofed village into shot.
Down there the shafts were scrawled with hooves

and hands fumbling for breath, but even if
the whole shift turned to prayer light was too far
above and unconcerned. Their faces show now
in the hush of parlours momently swept clear

of birdsong, a fierce unison of hymns
each Sunday, and a soft deep fall of dust.

II. Plates

They stand composed, the ministers and brothers,
formal as shadows, carrying the dead
beside the wrung-out pithead gear or under
fists of smoke thrown clear from furnaces

a quarter-mile below. Only the widows
turning from the lens or children confused
and staring out of frame disturb the grace
which I imposed to temper grief's sharp poise.

Too many funerals paced through that one-street
town: three generations, husbands, sons, confined
to looks simmering out from phosphor salts.
The dead are etched into the living. Here

they touch us with the lightness of a dream.
They wait behind my eye, in my one room.

Mr. Universe

for Richard Bradford

is delivered after hours
when the last windows have gone dark
by a gang of Russians running from the mob,
talking sour about a tip
and not getting it. He comes
flat-pack: his ribs fold up like struts,
his legs are tightened into place
with allen keys (which aren't provided),
all of which allows his transport
in a box that once held tins of soup.
His chest has drawers into which you put
his heart, already wheezing blood,
and lungs, which are a pair of drooping wings
until you tune his diaphragm.
Then take his eyes out of their eggbox,
his pulsing brain from its tissue paper.
Plug them in: he goes,
he rises beaming like a king
into his stone demesne.
But something's wrong here. Look,
then do a double-take: this man
you've seen somewhere before.
His clothes fit just that bit too well.
He turns a face to you. It's yours.

The death and burial of Cock Robin

Walter Potter, taxidermist, 1835-1918

But when I think of it, the days
among copse and hedgerow
wringing the necks of birds
to leave the skin intact, the nights
in the deserted stable loft
twisting the skeletons of linnets
from wire by half an inch of tallow,
I am there again, nocking the sparrow's bow,
my fingers blotched with mercury. Then
it was a wonder, all the birds
under one canopy and fame
moved me at last to this museum,
my own house. But that half inch
is still my separation from the dark,
from the glass tears of birds
I fixed in parodies of flight.
At night I hear their psalms,
the shovel rattling on earth,
and further off the white owl's eyes
bulging like moons over a narrow grave.

A horse in the dark

Quiet, quiet: do not dream
it is the owl parting fronds
of starlight, the water
muttering in abandoned mines.

It is the stillness falling
and pooling, drop
after drop,

it is the clouds spooling past on wires.

Soon you will hear oaks
pushing their mouths to the soil's tap,
the rushes drinking
far down the hill.

The lidless quartz blinks
at the snap of a twig's shadow;

a nothing so breathless.
It champs at a giant sky.

Nocturne

Dan Dare battles a squid underwater
then I rewind the tape.
The sofa empty beside me
I stare, press play. Dan Dare
battles a squid underwater.
He doesn't come up for air.
The phone's shaking. I ignore it and rewind the tape:
somewhere a lipsticked blonde is saying
– yes, that's my hero there,
battling a squid underwater – but I don't care
so I rewind the tape.
He doesn't come up for air,
she waits, presses a cigarette
to a flaring Zippo, marries someone else.
I try not to think of her, Dan Dare
battles a squid underwater
and then I rewind the tape.
She dyes her hair to look like seaweed,
has kids and a divorce. He
doesn't come up for air.
The sofa empty beside me,
I rewind the tape. Nothing changes
except the squid battles Dan Dare.

At Srebrenica

the grass is tongues, the severed dead
a thousand fossil gongs. In spring
the snowdrops part the earth like fingers, grip
the astounded air like groves of hands.

Dead reckoning

Winter brought a lump to her throat, then yours,
time wouldn't stent. For six months you drove
the hundred miles each week to stand with her
on the same Humber foreshore that shipped
generations of your family, trawlermen, raiders,
into the dark of the North Sea.
Your father flew coastal command
and some of the silence of him
waiting for U-boats to break surface is in you,
swelling like the lump in her throat.
Her funeral in May: lost on my Lindisfarne
of manuscripts I didn't go but thought of you,
dead-reckoning over a quiet motorway
at four a.m, under the Latin stars.

Dream #7912

After the war I came back through a quiet city
to the house with the fairytale slant to its roof,
where a bomb had rocked half the street to sleep.

She smiled to see me, showed me her two dim rooms
and the May sunlight between the rafters of her other four.
So we sat on deckchairs in the litter of bricks she still called

a garden, drinking tea and looking up at telegraph wires
like strings in the smashed piano, and the conversation carefully
avoided events of the past three years, until it was time to leave.

Then she smiled again, the quick press of her body
against mine the flutter of a bird's skeleton –
and I was gone, with a red sky edging

over the old quarter, and the street children, laughing.

Moonrise

The crossing into night will have its toll:
and like an obol, over the empty streets
the moon will rise. The blue screen will console

mother and working girl, switching her role
on a businessman's whim, but today again
the crossing into night will have its toll.

Alone in sitting rooms men drink their dole,
grow narrow. But for their tired wives
the moon will rise, the blue screen will console.

Now women peer from bedsit windows, a bowl
of satellites and clouds their company, and know
the crossing into night will have its toll:

minds fall in pieces; but they are made whole
by white miles of corridor. Light side, dark side,
the moon will rise, the blue screen will console

those who are lost, those far out at sea
reading the sonar like a letter home.
The crossing into night will have its toll.
The moon will rise, the blue screen will console.

Strange memories of death

for Philip K. Dick

I remember walking into a gas station
in early spring, 1982, and John Dowland
was playing on the radio and I said
boy it's hot today and the manager
said it sure is. It was Tuesday.

That was the day I called my ex-wife
from the forecourt and said let's go
to the cabin by the lake like last summer
and she said no, Phil, we sold it in 1979
but how are you these days?
I said fine, actually I never
felt better, it's so warm today
it could be last summer already
and she said I'm sorry Phil and hung up.

So I went back to the manager
to pay for the gas so that I could drive
on up to Marin County where she lived
except the manager was Robert so I
said hi Robert and he said hi Phil, don't worry
about the gas I'll cover it and here's your cat.

And the cat said hi Phil it's Jane
and jumped right up on my shoulder
so I said hi Jane, how come you're a cat these days
and she said they kept me in a box
all these years and I cried and cried
to be let out and eventually I cried so much
I turned into a cat. But I said it's good
to see you Jane and I don't mind if you're a cat.

So then me and Jane went back to my car
to drive up to Marin County
when it started to rain hard, a hot rain
cutting through the warm air over the roadway
and I thought we would drown

but Jane said don't worry, we'll get there
and the rain swooped down like stars in our headlights.
And we got to Marin and I pulled up in the driveway
my wife was asleep so I went in quietly
and my jacket was soaked so I took it off and hung it in the hall.

And I went through to the bedroom but it was me in the bed,
made out of a million sparks of light all different colours
and I must have heard myself come in because I sat up
and said hi Phil, it's Tuesday, second of March
and isn't there something you should be remembering?

But I'd forgotten. I've been trying to remember ever since.

(Philip K. Dick died on the second of march, 1982: the title is taken from
one of the last short stories he completed. Robert is Robert A. Heinlein,
and Jane is Dick's twin sister who died when they were five weeks old.)

The survivors

after Tracey Herd

The ceiling's cumulonimbus of damp
spreading as evening settles, light
dwindling from the storm-tossed carpet;

distantly, a white shoe scudding
off the edge of the world,
the fallen teacup's bulk, slanting:

returning a thousand years after
as archaeologists, this will be
all we can find, missing

the tiny figures jumbled
against a ruined sea,
clinging to the wreckage of ourselves.

Epilogue

For the cosmonauts

I, Yuri Gagarin, having not seen God,
wake now to the scrollwork of a body,
to my own white fibres leafing into the bone:
know that beyond this dome of rain there is
only the nothing where the soul sweeps
out its parallax like a distant star and truth
brightens to X, to gamma, through a metal sail.

So I return to you, cramming your pockets
with the atmosphere and evening news,
fumbling for gardens in the moon's shadow,
in its waterfalls of silence. I wish for you
familiar towns, their piers and amusement arcades
unpeopled at dusk, the unicorn tumbling by
on china hooves behind the high walls
of parks, among congregating lamps.

May you find Earth rising there, between
your steepled hands. May your voyages
end. May you have a cold unfurling
of limbs each morning, when I am fallen
out of the world.

Einstein on the beach

Einstein at three a.m. falls
from the bare rooms of the paper to the cold gulls
clacking on the moon's teeth.
He frames the satellite in his looped fingers,
finds the noun of it suddenly heavy in his palm:
its name both time and place, its doubled faces
a history of stargazing: from Daedalus
turned out towards the dark
to Plato, Archimedes staring back at us
over the radio waves, Copernicus absorbed
in study of that immense sky,
the rays of Tycho navigating
over gravity's curve. Soviets, astrologers,
they are the counterpoise
on the metaphor's extremity,
the stone that Einstein weighs and throws
into the future's billion lights, the names
that will be a thousand years arriving.
But dawn comes. Einstein smiles
and turns for home, leaving the gulls
diving for a moon skimming the water,
the stars clearing the ocean in a single bound.

Acknowledgements

Acknowledgements are due to the editors of the following publications where some of these poems first appeared: *Poetry Wales, Oxford Poetry, the Rialto, The Times Literary Supplement, poetrydaily.net, qualm.com, The Mays Anthologies, The University of East Anglia Creative Writing Anthology, 2008.*